MW01613515

PREFACE

This book of devotionals is meant to provide an avenue of prayerful attitude, to put a meditative pause into the day, to be a kind of incentive to holy consecration. It is a handy little thing, as pleasant a companion for the leisure of travel and of walks as it is for the business of the home and office.

Please do not judge each separate word too critically, or count the possible repetition of sentiment, — are not all prayers, in one sense, characterized by a single dominant tone? And please do not try to discover some emphasis which might be made a subject for dispute.

Surely, prayer need not always be formally uttered, always prefaced by an exalted address, always followed by a dignified Amen. Not always need we close our eyes and fold our hands. Hymns have been sung in silence, have they not? And, thank God, there is such a thing as a constant consecration, a "praying without ceasing."

God bless this little book.

MARY'S CALL

P.O. Box 162
504 W. U.S. Hwy. 24
Salisbury, MO 65281

Phone: 6603885308
Email: maryscall@maryscall.com

www.maryscall.com

MARY'S CALL

Mary's Call is a small, not-for-profit family organization. Our ministry is to encourage prayer, especially the Rosary and Way of the Cross.

The original undertaking of Mary's Call was the production of a 15 decade Rosary tape with meditations plus six hymns. The first order for the tape was received on May 4, 1989 (Ascension Thursday).

We create Mary's Call unique books and have available bibles, rosaries, scapulars, religious books, plaques, and many other items and religious gifts. In order for items to be sold at the lowest price, every effort is made to keep production costs to a minimum and, at the same time, maintain exceptional standards.

Mary's Call remains a very small family organization and is able to operate only through the assistance (time, talent, and donations) of friends. We hope that you will receive many blessings as a result of joining us in this ministry of prayer.

Table of Contents

JANUARY

1. My Father, renew all things in me today. Give me a new sense of old responsibilities. Renew my love. Renew my faith. Give me the longing for a new heaven and a new earth.

2. Eternal God, I take refuge in Thy grace. Do not let me confront the world defenseless. May I feel that a fiery wall protects me. In Thy care I feel safe.

3. Merciful Father, let me go before Thee in holy reverence; teach me to see Thy presence everywhere; let me acknowledge Thy providence and love in all things. Accompany me wherever I go.

4. Merciful Lord, help me in my struggle against temptation. May the banner of victory grace every battlefield. Make me a valiant warrior for Christ.

5. Father of life, give me abundant living. Redeem me from indifference; make me effectual; let all in me live and praise Thy holy name. Grant me the energy of eternal life.

6. Savior of the world, I pray for all who build Thy kingdom. Pour Thy blessing upon those who witness for Thee among the poor and the lost, the mighty and the mean, in this country and in the whole world.

7. Father, I want my affections to be unstinted and my love abundant. May I be like a lavishly shading tree, so that weary travelers may find rest and refreshment with me.

8. My Father, I pray for the homes of our people. May parents everywhere beautifully embody holy living. Sanctify filial love. Convert our families into fountains of living faith.

9. Heavenly Father, I thank Thee because all good things come to me from Thee. Let me go to Thee gladly, then, as to a living source from which I may ceaselessly dip, in the name of Christ, my Redeemer. Fill my earthen vessel to the brim. May Thy superabundant grace be to me a seal of Thy fellowship with me.

10. My God, tell me which is my besetting sin. Help me watch, so that I may recognize its temptation when it beckons. Arm me for the conflict; strengthen me by Thy grace.

11. Father, grant that my influence upon others today may be a good one. Forbid that I should become an offense to any seeking soul. May my intercourse with others make them better and draw them nearer Thee.

12. Lord of light, illumine my spirit. Let Thy rays penetrate the secret places of my heart. Make me a child of light; show me my secret sins, and teach me to hate them. Purge my desires, and give me a pure heart.

13. My Father, direct me to the way of life. Show me that the broad way leads to slavery and that its appeal invites to eternal disaster. Help me to know and to love the good.

14. Heavenly Father, I want to live near Thee. Let me go before Thee as though I were seeing Thee face to face. Fix in me the certainty that all the hosts of heaven are with me.

15. Oh God, my Father, all things are possible to him who believes. Increase my faith. Let me master all difficulties in confidence. Strengthen me for life's duty by Thy power. Level mountainous difficulties. May my path be smooth.

16. Dear Father, give me generous affection and love that seeketh not its own. May I demand less and give more. Redeem me from the fetters of selfishness.

17. Christ, my King, I would be subservient to Thee in everything I do. Conform every thought and whim and fancy in me to Thy will. May my soul preciously revere Thee.

18. Savior, teach me to pray for those I do not love. Take the film from my eyes, so that I too may see good in my enemies. Help me to love them.

19. Almighty God, I thank Thee for having invited me into Thy fellowship. Teach me to pray unceasingly. Lose me from that bondage of temporal things which keeps me from appreciating Thee. Grant me the ample freedom of heavenly joy.

20. Father, I want to serve Thee freely, gladly. Too often, I take offense at obvious duty for Thee. Grant me unstinted eagerness to serve.

21. God of grace, I lift up my soul to Thee. Reanimate it with new vigor. Purge it of lethargy. May Thy spirit continuously innervate my being.

22. My Lord and God, make me faithful in little things. May I conscientiously fulfill Thy demands. Lord, strengthen my faith, and by strengthening it hallow my obedience.

23. My Father, I would know certainly that I am a child of Thy grace. Help me to love Thee more intensely, and may I see from an increasing fervor of faith that my sins have been forgiven.

24. Father, may Thy favor lavishly be upon Thy people today. Relieve the anxious; soften hard hearts; raise the dead to life.

25. Almighty God, I pray for those who, because they are upon the battlefield, especially sense their helplessness. May they know that Thou dost not forsake them. Show these how much Christ has done for them, and grant them a royal victory for His sake.

26. My Father, inspire the spirit of gratitude in me. Keep me from accepting the astounding gift of Thy grace as though I had deserved it. May I each day again praise Thee for Thy strange compassion.

27. Great God, lead me into all truth. Guard me against obstinacy and self-assertion. May I be receptive to Thy truth, and seek and love Thy light more than all things.

28. Father, show me the purpose of my life on earth. Teach me the preciousness of time. May every hour of my life, and every day reveal resplendent praise.

29. Dear Lord, I can live on earth, but only by sometimes breathing the atmosphere of eternity. May the invigorating winds of God's holy hill often blow upon this stifling plain and give me new strength.

30. Merciful God, teach me to appreciate Thy compassion fully. Make me know that condescending sympathy is the secret of real strength. Let me manifest that strength by supporting the frailty of others. May I feel honored by the privilege of bearing a fellow's burden.

31. Father, I thank Thee for my daily bread. May I enjoy it appreciatively and gratefully. Give me the bread of life, and let me by its nourishment grow in grace and sanctification.

FEBRUARY

1. My Lord, Thou hast graciously permitted me to begin another month. May I begin it and end it in Thy service and in Thy praise. Help me to keep Thy commandments and to find my happiness in keeping them.

2. Almighty God, may Thy will be mine. Let me desire nothing outside of Thee. May all other joys be bitter to my taste. May I desire only what is holy, and be happy only in what is good.

3. My Father, show me my sins as they are when revealed in the light of Thy countenance and not as they seem in the appraisal of men. Only in Thy light can I actually see things as they are. Cast that light upon my sins. Then they will shock me and I will hate them.

4. Father, give me access to Thy abundance for all my needs. Let Thy stars illumine my night; Thy angels comfort my frequent imprisonments.

5. Savior, remind me always and in all things of Thy holy example. May the words I speak be lovable, the friendliness I manifest be hallowed, and my intolerance be mitigated. Give me Thy mind, Christ Jesus.

6. My Lord and my God, I want to glorify and honor Thee. Expel from me any desire that does not please Thee. Free me from selfishness, and enable me to live unembarrassed in Thy light.

7. Holy Father, may I seize upon the inheritance I have in Christ Jesus. May I share in my Savior's inexhaustible riches. Clothe me in fine garments, put shoes on my feet, so that I may witness for the gospel appropriately,

8. Father, if there is in me this day some unclean thought, purge me of it. If I should desire something that would offend another, quench it by Thy grace.

9. My God, I thank Thee for this new day and for all the grace Thou wilt give me in it. May it not be a fruitless day for me. Teach me to receive what Thou wouldst have me learn. And may I tomorrow see the profit of this day's experience.

10. Merciful Lord, may my profession of discipleship be more than an empty sound. I would that those I meet today may see that I follow Thee. Make me friendly, sympathetic, upright.

11. Father, what wouldst Thou teach me today? I want to understand it very clearly. Make me sensitively aware of Thy voice. Help me to recognize the truth amid overwhelming falsehood and to cling loyally to Thy gospel.

12. Heavenly Father, heal my soul. Protect me from the venom of the world. Keep me from inclining increasingly to evil. If Thou dost heal me, Lord, I shall be really well.

13. Heavenly Father, enrich me with the knowledge of Thy truth. Impart new energy to me each day from Thy word. Keep me from trivial and mean thoughts that would ravage my spirit and lay waste my life. Give me the mind of Christ.

14. My Father, I thank Thee for all the benefits of this life. May I see them, count them, and so make my life a constant sacrifice of praise.

15. O God, my Father, deliver me from the restlessness of this world and fill my heart with love for and reverent fear of Thee. Forbid that I be torn by conflicting loyalties. May I long for Thee and for Thee alone unceasingly.

16. Almighty God, may Thy word be my guide. I want to cling to it even when I find it difficult to obey. Help me to take the right road, even though it be hard and thorny. Thy will be done.

17. My Father, teach me to pray without ceasing. Grant that my fellowship with Thee may continue undisturbed. Enable me to abide in Thee. Let me live in the shadow of Thy wings.

18. Great God, give me a compassionate heart. Allow me to treat the world's wounds tenderly. Keep me from unholy austerity and unsympathetic judgments.

19. Holy Spirit, keep my memory sensitively active so that I may think of Thy many benedictions and thank Thee for them often; so that I may recall my sins and remain humble; so that I may frequently be reminded of Thy mercy and hope in Thee. Keep my eyes steadfastly fixed upon the hills.

20. My Father, let Thy holy spirit accompany me today and be active in me. Make each of my days a Sabbath of unprofaned consecration. Help me to dedicate every act of my life to Thee.

21. Almighty God, may the rays of Thy goodness vivify my spirit. Keep me from indifference and inertness. Baptize me with the Holy Ghost and with fire

22. Gracious God, in confident faith and expectation I lift up my eyes to Thee. Let me walk with Thee today in a tender and close fellowship. Thy word be my light and Thy grace my strength. In the strength of Thy love, I would love my neighbors.

23. Father, I yearn to delight in Thee. I would not only follow Thee but would follow Thee gladly. May Thy law be my delight and Thy will my happiness.

24. Father in Heaven, bind me to my brethren with strong and holy bonds. Keep me from everything that leads to estrangement from them. May my thoughts and words be of service to Thee and all Thy children. May all that is in me conduce to make Thy great family a single home.

25. Lord, my God, assure me of Thy forgiveness. Give that I may now abhor the sins Thou hast forgiven and henceforth always shun them.

26. Heavenly Father, let Thy grace rest upon me. May I experience something of Thy strength today. Free me from the solitude of selfishness, and help me to stay in Thy amiable fellowship.

27. Heavenly Father, Thy mercy is upon all Thy creatures. May it be upon me also. Help me to appreciate the marvelous grace that sustains my life. Convince me that I live from day to day simply because of Thy goodness.

28. Holy Father, let Thy light shine in my soul today also. May the wonder of Thy gospel grow in my estimation constantly, and make me yield to it completely. Nourish me with the bread of life.

29. My Father, let me, too, contribute to the coming of Thy kingdom. Forbid that I by my conformity to the world should restrain the fruitfulness of Thy truth. Make me a real servant of Christ.

MARCH

1. Merciful Lord, I praise and thank Thee for giving my daily work, apparently so insignificant, an eternal value. May I do that work in the confident hope of immortality. Grant that especially the little duties of life may also serve Thy purpose. May Christ in all things live in me.

2. Father of all things living, strengthen the social life of all Thy people. Unify their hearts; unify them by the consciousness of their common needs, and by their common rejoicing in the same Redeemer.

3. My Lord, forgive in me everything in which I have thus far failed, and bless what I have done that was pleasing to Thee. Help me to remain loyal. May the end of my life be better than the beginning, so that when twilight falls I may first become aware of the light of dawn.

4. Father, help me to stay in the shadow of the Almighty when I threaten to become restless and irritable. Give me peace and repose even in the center of conflict and of temptation.

5. My Lord and Savior, enable me to follow Thee sincerely this whole day. May I not dread the cross Thou givest me, but bear it willingly. Make me lose my life, in order that I may really find it.

6. Merciful God, I thank Thee for everything that makes life pleasant. Thou hast lavished an abundance of undeserved benefits upon me. I thank Thee for the friendliness of others, for all people in whom the spirit of love and sympathy resides.

7. Heavenly Father, I want to feel Thy presence. May I be as aware of Thy nearness as of that of some human friend. Grant that I may taste the sweetness of fellowship with Thee. And may I never lose it.

8. Dear Lord, deliver me from slavish dread. Prevent my life from being paralyzed by unbelief. Keep adversity and Cares from becoming a curse to me. May I always abide in Thee.

9. O Lord my God, I would be a branch of the true vine. I want to glorify Thee by bearing much fruit. May men see my good works, may the poor and heavily burdened derive encouragement and comfort from my life.

10. Almighty God, I wish to begin this day's work with Thee. Support my frailty with Thy strength, so that I may with gladness realize Thy will.

11. My Father, do Thou direct my life today. Stand guard at the gates of my senses. Show me what to see and hear. Make my thoughts also subservient to Thee. Incline my ear to understand Thy word.

12. O Lord, my God, give me the blissful assurance that I have been reconciled with Thee through my Savior. May I remain a child in my Father's house. Accept me into Thy holy fellowship and let me share in the abundance of Thy table.

13. Father, may my work be a consecrated serving of Thee. Hallow and purify my tasks today, so these may at last bless my soul.

14. Savior, make me tender hearted and sincerely humble. Give me a quiet spirit. Free me from inner restiveness and uncertainty. Grant me Thy peace.

15. Spirit of Love, illumine all those who are influential in our country. Reveal Thy truth especially to those who speak and write, so that a purifying and uplifting influence may proceed from them.

16. Merciful God, show me how I can make this world's suffering more endurable. Help me today to make the burden of some fellow man less oppressive. May I heal the wounded heart.

17. Father, gladly would I surrender all to Thee. Give me clean thoughts, tender feelings, and a righteous will.

18. Heavenly Father, keep my mind bent upon Thy will, in order that I may fear Thy name. Make obedient in me all that haughtily resists Thy purposes, lest discord cruelly distort the perfect harmony.

19. Eternal God, transform the winter of my life into spring. Do Thou by the warmth of Thy grace melt the coldness of my love. I would flourish and bear abundant fruit for Thee.

20. Holy Spirit, enable me evermore completely to surrender myself. Let Thy grace move in me unhampered. May Thy kingdom come to me, and may it through me come to others.

21. My Savior, make me a child of light. Keep me from fretting and complaining. May I never become subject to gloom, to somber heaviness of spirit. FM me with hope and gladness, and may others derive new courage from my happy confidence.

22. O Prince of Peace, do Thou put an end to the wars of men. Take conflict out of human affairs. Free us from bitterness, and purge us of mistrust and suspicion.

23. My Father, show me Thy glory to the extent my eyes can bear to see it. Reveal something of Thy beauty to my soul, and so lead me to profounder obeisance and a more complete surrender.

24. Eternal God, when Thou dolt will it, Thou canst purify me. Make me really know that Thou canst heal even the leprous body. Assure me that by Jesus' strength the pollution of the world can be cleansed. Create a pure heart in me, O Lord, and renew in me a steadfast spirit.

25. God of love, teach me to bear my cross. May I not try to evade it, nor to choose the easy way of personal impulse. Help me to choose the way of duty, even though it means oppression and sacrifice.

26. Eternal God, may all I attempt be consecrated to Thee. Renew my spirit, so that with a heavenly disposition I may dispose of earthly tasks. May I earnestly seek the things above.

27. Father of all men, hear me as I pray for my brethren in the whole world. May the light of the cross be bright before their eyes and illuminating in their hearts. And may their burdens be light.

28. Merciful, crucified Savior, may I remember Thy grief when temptations come to me. Teach me to hate the sin that grieves Thee. Let me emerge a victor from every battle with temptation.

29. My Father, may Thy favor fall upon the little responsibilities of this day, so that these too may share in a heavenly purposiveness. May I know that a divine blessing rests upon the simplest and least significant of tasks.

30. Eternal God, Thou hast been marvelously patient with me. May I now be patient with others. Show me the blessing of humbly bearing ills. And may I not confuse Thy purposes by imposing my own thoughts upon them. Help me to rest in and to wait upon Thee.

31. Merciful Saviour, do Thou gather the pitiful fragments of my life and create of them something that pleases Thee. Forgive my infidelity. Forgive what I have neglected to do. May Thy mercy and Thy kindness sustain me.

APRIL

1. Heavenly Father, open my eyes to the miracle of Thy goodness. Thy benefits, the rich gifts of Thy grace have become matters of course to me. Grant, Lord, that I may again acknowledge the miraculous in Thy favors. Then I shall praise and glorify Thee for each day's privileges.

2. Merciful God, I believe that Thou art Lord. Support my unbelief, lest this concession be a matter of words merely. May I be Thy subject in all that I do let me obey no will but Thine. Thy will be done.

3. My risen Lord and Savior, induce me to think upon Thy crucifixion today. Lord Jesus, may I bear Thy dying in my own body. May Thy passion and death affect my soul profoundly and fill me with a humble and holy earnestness.

4. Gracious Lord, include my polluted and lost life within the pale of Thy gracious pardon. Redeem me from the power of sin. Acquit me of guilt and give me Thy blessed peace.

5. Merciful Father, bestow upon me the spirit of kindness. Save me from harshness, impatience, and haughtiness. Enable me to use Thy strength to help my neighbor to bear his cross.

6. My Savior, conform me to Thy death, so that I may also experience the power of Thy resurrection. Raise me from the grave to a new life. May today be a beautiful Easter for me.

7. Heavenly Father, in Thy grace grant me everything I need. Keep me from becoming anxious for the morrow. May I serve Thee today simply, in faithful obedience, and may Christ truly live in me.

8. Savior, Thou knowest the stress and travail of life's work upon earth. Bless my toil also, and make it successful. May labor for Thee, and present my accomplishments to Thee as a sacrifice of praise. Keep me from dishonesty. Make me trustworthy and upright.

9. Heavenly Father, guard my eternal inheritance for me, lest I lose it, and remain outside of the fellowship with Thee to which Thou hast opened the way. May I find my home in Thee. Grant me the gladness and the liberty Thy children enjoy.

10. Lord Jesus, my Savior, let me be raised with Thee today from the grave of sin. May my going to and fro be with Thee in heaven. Lift me into Thy marvelous light, and let me see Thy glory.

11. Eternal God, the God of hope, send down Thy light upon me, and cause it to dispel the doubts and fears amid which I grope. May I acknowledge Thee as the light of life.

12. O my Savior, early in the morning I would sing songs to Thee. May I in glad obedience be always filled with hymns of Praise. Forbid that my uncongenially and unfriendliness should bar others from following Thee.

13. Risen Lord and Savior, may I grow in Thy grace and knowledge. Lead me into a fuller appreciation of the mystery of Thy life and death. Let me rise with Thee into a new life.

14. My Savior, I praise Thee because Thou hast wrought life and immortality for me. I thank Thee for having removed the veil. Lead me to live, then, as becomes a child of the eternal God. Make me worthy to be called Thy child.

15. Heavenly Father, assure me of my adoption, and may the awareness of being Thy child be so beautiful and dear to me that I live worthily of this high calling. Forbid that I should ever voluntarily turn to sin again. May I demonstrate that I am a child of the King.

16. Eternal God, I would hear Thy voice today. May that voice sound clear through all the noises of this world. And may I hear it not only in the secrecy and the quiet of my room, but also amid the confusion of affairs.

17. My risen Lord, I would experience the power of Thy resurrection. Raise me above the hubbub of this world. Lift me to the plane of the life of heaven. So let me prove a blessing to others.

18. My Father, this day I pray that I may willingly obey Thee. May my duty be my delight and Thy law my gratification.

19. Holy Father, make me a child of hope. Banish from me oppressive doubt and belief. Let me rejoice in Thy light. Make me look confidently to the dawn when I walk in the valley of the shadow. And may men see that I have been with Christ.

20. Merciful God, light in me the ardent fire of hallowed love. Forbid that the spirit of this world extinguish the flame. May it shine flourishingly, and may I be faithful unto Thee until death.

21. Holy Father, I would find rest with Thee. Eagerly would I quit the conflict of life in favor of entering Thy peace. Redeem me from all that hampers my entering into rest. Expel every wicked wish and unwarranted anxiety.

22. Holy God, I dedicate my body to Thee. Never let me forget that it is a temple of the Holy Ghost. Teach me moderation. Make me know that the laws of health are also Thy commandments.

23. God of Strength, arm me for this day's conflict. Keep me from fainting in the first encounter. Grant me victory over every tempter. May I be more than conqueror in Christ.

24. Heavenly Father, condescend to Thy people. Show them Thy glory and Thy truth amid the falsehood that surrounds them. Have compassion upon the many who do not want to know Thee. Inspire in them a longing for holiness and place their feet upon the path of peace.

25. My Father, may men be more fraternally disposed. May I, too, be delivered from the bondage of selfish interest. Give me the liberty of love. Broaden my affections and let me serve Thee by serving my neighbors.

26. Holy Father, teach me to hate sin. Fix my mind upon things good and pure. Always reveal more of Thy sublime beauty to me and conform me to Thy image.

27. Holy Ghost, illumine my thoughts, and clarify my understanding, so that I may discern rightly that which is good and that which is evil. Only in Thy light can I see things truly. I would walk in that light.

28. Father in Heaven, may I see Thy radiant throne from afar. May my life reveal the virtue of profound reverence for Thee. May I go upon earth as one who knows heavenly glory. Forbid that I should squander my years in indolence.

29. Lord my God, now this day's work begins again. May every motive I have in mind in going about it be pure, may every purpose I would realize deserve Thy eager benediction.

30. Merciful Father, let not this month pass without my being really reconciled to Thee. Forgive my disobedience and my carelessness. Wash me clean by Thy grace. I would begin the new month with a pure heart.

MAY

1. O God, lift me Into Thy glorious light, lest I grope perpetually. Cheer my heart and spirit by Thy illuminating grace. Inflame my thoughts and words and deeds, so that from my animation men may see that I am Thy happy child.

2. Heavenly Father, I thank Thee for Thy care of me. Thy mercy is inexhaustible. Thou don bless this day also with Thy goodness. Help me to note Thy innumerable blessings. Free me from spiritual blindness. May I acknowledge Thy presence everywhere.

3. Holy God, May the beauty of spring make me praise and glorify Thee, my Creator and Redeemer. Break the power of winter in my soul. Grant me Thy spirit, in order that he may expel the frost and cold, and may make room in me for the warmth and gladness of the Lord.

4. Father in Heaven, show me the significance of little things. May I praise Thee by means of them. Teach me to take every moment of this day into the light of Thy presence. So may my whole life be presented as a sacrifice to Thee.

5. Merciful God, make my spirit tender and sympathetic by Thy grace. Redeem me from the coldness of worldly love, and from the mercilessness of pride. Grant me the spirit of Jesus.

6. God, my Father, help me to walk the path of life with confident steps. Invigorate Thy child when he is tired strengthen his feet when they falter. So may I bravely take the field in battle for my King.

7. Heavenly Father, grant me the grace of helping to extend brotherly love among men by my life. May the gulf that separates factions not ever be broadened by me. Instead, may I cause friendship and trust to flourish.

8. Dear Lord, support me in my attempts to do bravely and aggressively what is naturally difficult and unpleasant to do. May even my disappointments prove a blessing to me.

9. My Father, help me to radiate a good and friendly spirit today. May I by a poised faith encourage the tremulous and quicken the disappointed. May my inner happiness prove contagious to others.

10. My Father, never let me forget that also in grief Thou wilt not forsake me but be at my side. Thou knowest what is profitable to me, and knowest what I can bear.

11. Eternal God, Thy blessing is my boon, and in Thy peace, I find rest. Therefore, I pray: be merciful to me. Let me share in Thy divine gifts. Strengthen me by Thy word for this day's toil.

12. My Father, teach me to see the eternal in temporal things. May I penetrate to things real through things apparent May I thus apprehend Thy spirit in the letter of Thy word. Teach me to acknowledge Thee in all things.

13. Almighty God, lift upon me the light of Thy countenance. Let the love of my Lord gladden my heart. May I not desire human praise but only long to please my King. Thy will be done.

14. Father of Light, I thank Thee for everyone who reprimands or warns me and for everyone who by spoken or written words increases my knowledge. Praise and gratitude be Thine for all that makes life rich.

15. Father of all grace, I thank Thee for my daily bread. May I receive it as from Thy hand and not as though I earned it. Let it be to me a token of Thy grace, and may I enjoy it as such, humbly and gratefully.

16. Father, I reveal my sins before Thy presence. Annihilate the power of evil in my soul, and blot from Thy holy book every transgression I have committed against Thee.

17. Merciful God, I pray for all young Christians. Strengthen them for their difficulties. May they not be overwhelmed by the tempter's power. And may their life mature in the light of Thy grace.

18. Holy Ghost, I pray that Thou wilt reside in me. Lead me into all truth. Give me a glimpse of eternal glory. May the commandments of the Lord be my delight, and make me a faithful follower of Christ.

19. O Lord, give me a vital and sure awareness of the fact that I am a child of God. Help me to think so highly of that adoption that I may never do anything mean or unworthy. Keep my foot from sliding.

20. Merciful God, today, too, I would be a child of light. Keep me in Thy fellowship. Teach me to appreciate the riches of my inheritance in Christ. May I go on my way, clothed in the wedding garment of Thy kingdom.

21. Gracious Spirit, shape my soul. Make it receptive to divine influences. May I see Thy activities everywhere. May I be able to hear Thy softest whisper.

22. Savior of the World, I pray for all those who preach Thy name. Make them strong by Thy grace, in order that their message may reveal Thy power. Show them Thy glory, and they will execute their calling with gladness. Grant that the world may accept their testimony.

23. My Father, show me how I can truly serve Thee. Keep me from separating myself from others. May I know the happiness of self-denial and gladly and sincerely seek my neighbor's welfare.

24. Holy Spirit, make my fellowship with Thee constantly more intimate. I am not satisfied with merely knowing the truth but would also hunger after Thee with ardent love. Reveal to me the mystery of Thy dear presence.

25. My Father, shed the beautiful light of Thy gospel upon my soul. May that heavenly seed sprout in me, flourish, and soon yield abundant fruit.

26. Holy Father, I dedicate to Thee the labor of this day. Stamp Jesus' seal upon it. Purge it of selfish motives, lest my daily work harm my brethren.

27. My Father, let me expect great things today. May I not let myself drift through life purposelessly. Teach me to keep my eyes upon the Lord, to see Him in all that is good and beautiful, and to love his appearing.

28. My Father, deliver me from any fear that might lay waste my powers. Teach me to fear only what is sinful. Make me a bold aggressive defender of the truth.

29. Gracious God, let me go before Thee today in a way that pleases Thee. Increase in me the certainty of my adoption, and help me to present to Thee a life, which appropriately fulfills its high calling.

30. My God, I pray for Thy kingdom. Make me love it more fervently and defend it more faithfully. Manifest Thy power in me, in order that I may be glad to testify for Thee. Let me taste the sweetness of Thy kingdom, so that I may eagerly tell others of it.

31. Holy Ghost, Thou hast rich gifts for the children of men: gifts of peace, of joy, and of rest. I come now, poverty stricken, without money, without strength. Give me these riches of Thy grace and I shall have abundance eternally.

JUNE

1. Great God, I want this to be a month of flourishing spiritual growth for me. Make me heavenly minded. Forbid that I should ever stoop to what is mean and base. Instead may I in Thy strength seek the things that are above.

2. Holy Spirit let me feel Thy presence in me today. May it be a fellowship existing not in beautiful phrases but in a blessed reality. I would rejoice in Thee and be glad in Thy strength. Show me everything in Thy light.

3. Heavenly Father, make me faithful in intercessory prayer. May I suffer with those that are oppressed and rejoice with those that are glad. Make me wrestle with Thee for human souls and lead me to intervene for them before the throne of grace.

4. Holy Spirit, sanctify my whole life. May my daily work, too, be a kind of prayer offered to Thee. Use it to make me better. Lead me to hunger and thirst after righteousness.

5. Lord Jesus, all power is in Thee. Grant me Thy strength, then, and enable me by it to really pray. Loose me from temporal interests, help me to concentrate upon eternal things. I would have my secret fellowship with Thee, O Savior, become the absorbing reality of my life.

37

6. Heavenly Father, make my soul be like a beautiful garden. Keep it from dearth and sterility. May my godliness flourish in Thee and yield choice fruits.

7. My Father, let this day prove profitable to me for eternity; set in clearer relief my responsibilities to Thee; and give me a greater assurance of being Thy child.

8. Heavenly Father, I thank Thee because Thy love is inexhaustible. Teach me to know that it bears me up and gives me energy for my tasks. I thank Thee, too, For Thy mercy. Fill me with an increasing self-denying surrender to Thy holy will.

9. Holy Spirit, I thank Thee for the radiance of this morning. I would that its brilliance were an image of my soul. Let the light of eternity penetrate my heart. Then I shall be glad and proclaim the beauties of my God.

10. My Father, teach me to do Thy will. Forbid that I should counteract Thy purposes by my own folly. May my words be acceptable, and may others by them be attracted to Thee.

11. Holy Father, I want to live before Thee in quiet reverence. May my happy hours, too, be full of hallowed fear. May I not forget that I am a child of the Most High even in moments of jest and jollity. Let Christ live in me.

12. Great and mighty God, let the sense of Thy power outweigh in me the sense of my own weakness. Do not let me confront the enemy helplessly; equip me for the encounter by Thy marvelous race. Help me to conquer in Christ.

13. My Savior, let Thy Holy Spirit penetrate my being today and heal my soul by His gracious influence. Help me to live in the fear of the Lord.

14. Gracious God, keep me near Thee today. May all my energies be rooted in Thee, and all I do be permeated by Thy divine grace. I pray that all my words may breathe Thy spirit.

15. My Father, teach me to worship Thee in spirit and in truth. May I approach Thee always in holy reverence and awe. Let my life bear abundant fruit for Thy glory.

16. Merciful God, let me walk with Thee today, and let me do it in appropriate dress. Give me a wedding garment. May my words be seven times purged by Thy holy fire, so that I may be worthy to be called Thy friend.

17. Merciful Father, reveal to me my secret faults. Redeem me from the sins of which I am not aware. Make me honest with myself. Wash me clean of hidden unrighteousness.

18. My Savior, allow me to live in a state of holy fellowship with Thee throughout this day. May I learn to know the mystery of the Lord: reveal to me the hidden riches of Thy glory. Give me a pure heart, and I shall see God.

19. Merciful Lord, help me more completely to love the noble and the good. Take the scales from my eyes in order that I may see things as Thou seest them. Give me the mind of Christ.

20. Almighty God, strengthen me by Thy peace. Deliver me from all harmful anxiety and doubt. Direct all my powers upon the one end of doing Thy will. Then I shall bear rich fruits increasingly.

21. Father, grant that I may in Christ Jesus grow in Thy knowledge. Reveal His beauty to me in my daily work. Give me a consuming need for His indwelling grace.

22. Heavenly Father, give me Thy grace in order that I may hate all sin. Thou knowest that I sometimes secretly long for what is evil. Grant me a new spirit, so that I may sincerely abhor sin.

23. Holy Father, bless me, for I would be a blessing to others. May streams of living water proceed from me. May I impart to the discouraged lives of others something of true joy. Make me a fountain of pure water for thirsty pilgrims.

24. Eternal God, I thank Thee for having made Thy earth so beautiful. I praise Thee because all that is about me proclaims Thy majesty. Open my eyes to the grandeur of God. Impart to my soul the spirit of worship. So will the beauty of the world lead me to Thee.

25. Father, do not allow the world to impress its seal upon me. Equip me instead by Thy grace to help in rejuvenating the world and in making it conform to Thy image.

26. Great God, teach me to go before Thee with a holy awe. Keep me from idle chatter and superficiality in my prayers to Thee. May I kneel before Thee always with a becoming spirit. Reveal the radiance of Thy throne to me from afar.

27. My Lord and God, may this day begin and end favorably for me. Consecrate again the broken fragments of pious resolutions, so that I may conclude this day in complete surrender to Thee.

28. My Father, send me Thy Spirit to accompany me each hour of this day. May He illuminate my thoughts, inspire me, and teach me what to think and say. May I not grieve Him by my words or deeds.

29. Almighty God, lead me according to Thy counsel. Direct me so that I may not confuse my life by foolish motives. May I ever look up to Thee. Teach me to know Thee intimately and to follow Thee.

30. God of love, abide with me in life's dark moments. May these moments be my friends and not my enemies. May grief and sorrow increase my heavenly heritage. May temporal difficulties shape me for eternal glory.

JULY

1. Merciful God, I lift up my heart to Thee. May I remain all day upon the high plane of fellowship with Thee. Forbid that my thoughts should stoop to consider unworthy things. May my dwelling be in the heavens, and may the motives inspired by Thy grace completely dominate my thought.

2. Eternal Father, fountain of light and peace, grant me and all who worship Thee blessed rest today. Convert my anxiousness into confident trust, my fear into content, my restlessness into the bliss of communion with Thee.

3. Heavenly Father, keep my eye trained upon Thee as I go about earning my daily bread. Save me from pursuing things that are common and passing. Keep me from seeking my crown in the dust. May I long earnestly for the things that are above.

4. Great God, I thank Thee for my country. Bless our President and our Congress. May the dew of Thy grace rest upon us as a nation. May we love Thee more loyally and therefore love our country.

5. Gracious God, make me compassionate, even as Thou art. Make me tenderhearted and lovingly sympathetic to all those who grieve or are heavily burdened. Enable me to give comfort and encouragement to Thy suffering disciples.

6. My God, I offer Thee my life with all of its defects and its pollution. Have pity upon me. Deliver me from doubt and give me that crying need for Thee that leads to a complete surrender to Thy holy will.

7. Heavenly Father, how beautiful are Thy works in all places. Thou? naked the grass to grow upon the hills, and fillest every valley with flowers. The whole earth is full of Thy glory. Dazzle me with Thy beauty, until I conform myself to Thy glorious image.

8. Almighty God, fountain of all blessing, do Thou graciously lift up my heart unto Thee. May I care profoundly to be of the same mind as Thou art. Do Thou rule all my thoughts and renew all my desires.

9. Father of all mercy, grant that Thy spirit may reign over us. May those in authority everywhere be subject to Thee. May all whom Thou hest ordained to power strive only for what pleases and praises Thee.

44

10. Father, help me to glorify and honor Thy holy name. Make me acknowledge Thy favors; may a note of holy joy ever resound more clearly in my soul. Place a new song upon my lips this day, dear Lord.

11. Holy Spirit, remind me of the many things I too easily forget. Sanctify my memory so that I may retain good things and lose no treasures. Grant that I may not have to relearn today what I was taught yesterday.

12. My Father, give me the indubitable assurances of a victorious life. May I never despair because of my many faults; may I, instead, derive new courage from the treasures of Thy grace.

13. My Father, keep Heaven constantly open before me. Give me an ample vision of Thy glory. Renew the glimpse of it until I long for it passionately. May these glimpses of eternal bliss be my sustenance day and night.

14. Savior, make me one of Thy faithful disciples, lest I leave Thee in the hour of trial. May I willingly prefer bearing my cross upon the narrow way to following the ease and pleasure of the broad road. Crucify me with Thee.

15. My Father, may the end of my journey be more beautiful than its beginning. May the night of my life be illumined by Thy radiant grace. Send Thy forgiving love to banish every cloud. Lord, I would renew my covenant with Thee today.

16. My dear Father, help me to do Thy will. Show me all things plainly in Thy light. Set me free from the works of darkness, from all that cannot resist the light. Grant me Thy divine life, so that I may truly serve my brethren.

17. God, Eternal Light, graciously illumine my spirit. Be with me when darkness lowers, when my energies threaten to wane. Thy Spirit support me, so that I may live and walk as a child of light.

18. Father, teach me gratitude. Show me the riches of Thy grace, so that I may unceasingly praise and glorify Thee. Deliver me from the spirit of discontent.

19. Father, may I never forget that I am a member in a great family. May my life contribute to the happiness of its members. Forbid that any one of them should lack in comfort or joy because of my infidelity, that any should have to be poverty stricken because I have failed in my duty. Enable me to help others.

20. Eternal God, let me experience some of the potentialities of eternal life. May the hope of immortal glory strengthen my faith and perseverance, in order that I may see clearly and never tire of my great purpose in life.

21. Father, help me to believe in the power of the invisible world. When earth seems so terribly real and that other world so vaguely aloof, reveal to me, then, Thy irresistible might. I pray of Thee that thou wilt make me doubly sure of that spiritual reality. Let me rest and trust in Thee.

22. Heavenly Father, incline my heart to keep Thy commandments; deliver me of everything that deflects my attention from the good. Make me thoroughly honest and perfectly pure, even though no eye but Thine may see.

23. God of all strength, graciously condescend to support my weakness. Let not sin defeat me, but do Thou arm me against it in Thy great power. Make me unconquerable by Thy grace.

24. Merciful God, I thank Thee for Thy Word. Help me to appropriate its riches unto myself. May Thy promises strengthen my faith. Then I shall energetically run the course laid out for me, steadily keeping my eyes upon Jesus.

25. Father, again I pray that Thou wilt make me heavenly minded. Keep me in Jesus' fellowship. May His attractiveness enamor me and induce me to yield to Him completely.

26. Merciful Father, help me to believe that, inadequate as I am, I can do great things in Christ. Never allow me to be submerged by earthly care, but make me a child of immortal hope. May I visibly see that I am approximating more closely the great aim of my life.

27. Father, renew my gratitude each morning. Teach me to appreciate Thy grace more fully, lest songs of praise die on my lips. Make me Thy joyful child.

28. My Father, I thirst for the water of life. Let it issue from me today in abundance, cleansing me of my sin, refreshing me for good motives, quickening my purposes. Convert me into a blossoming garden.

29. O Lord, help me to rest in Thee today. Keep me from impatience. May I quietly await upon Thy works until the pillar of cloud moves. Then I shall follow in confidence.

30. Merciful Father, I pray for all whose lives abound in suffering and disappointment, who never baste the sweetness of temporal prosperity. Bless them. Keep their hearts from bitterness. May Thy fellowship be to them an immeasurably adequate compensation.

31. My Father, assure me of Thy complete forgiveness. May the sins of yesterday not confront me again today. Cleanse me of guilt and help me to hate evil. May I stand before Thee robed in the white garment of righteousness.

AUGUST

1. O Lord my God, may I sense Thy living presence. Make my soul aware of the slightest whisper of Thy voice. May I hear the carillons of eternity sounding clear above the noises of the world. Make me to walk in heaven even here on earth.

2. Compassionate God, send me Thy mercy. Fill me with joy and gladness. Banish all harshness and bitterness from my disposition. May my heart manifest the fruits of the spirit in praise of Thy holy name.

3. Father let me rejoice in the beauty of summer. May its glory excite in me a longing for the perfect life. May the blossoms of the Spirit color my life.

4. My Father, let nothing overwhelm me. Keep prosperity from proving poison to my soul, adversity from embittering my spirit. Let all things issue in my welfare and reflect Thy glory.

5. Father in Heaven, be Thou my refuge from my enemies. Keep me steadfast in the hour of temptation and fearless in the face of danger. Send me Thy peace as a token of my belonging to Thee.

6. Heavenly Father, let me do something, be it ever so small an achievement, in praise of Thee today. I pray that my work may bless others. Permeate what I say and do with holy energy. Make me a striking image of my Lord.

7. Father, help me to hear the Master's voice today, whether it call me to an unwelcome duty or ask me to perform some pleasant task.

8. My God and Father, let the work of this whole day be dedicated to Thee. Shamefacedly I confess that my daily con‑ duct sometimes profanes my discipleship. Grant me Thy spirit so that my labor may be consecrated to Thee. Make me a fit instrument by Thy grace.

9. O Holy Spirit, infuse into my soul the atmosphere of Heaven. Cause evil in me to die and good to flourish. Adorn me in celestial beauty. May my whole life be glorified by Thy grace.

10. Merciful God, I pray that my life may yield fruit unceasingly. May I reap benefits even from sorrow and disappointment, and may my faults prove a boon to me. Let every grief and every sad experience issue in Thy glory.

11. O God and Father, I would hunger and thirst after Thee. Fill my soul with a holy yearning when I grow indifferent to prayer. Grant me Thy peace and share with me Thy power.

12. Merciful God may Thy creation proclaim Thy glory to me and may the beauty of nature fill me with love and awe. Grant that the sublimity of the firmament may direct and attract me to the greater glory of my Master.

13. Dear Lord, sanctify my lips so that my words may be loving and my attitude encouraging to my neighbors.

14. Almighty God, I thank Thee for Thy willingness to share with me Thy fellowship. Do Thou speak to me when I fail to speak. Come to me when I remain afar, and reveal Thy grace to me when I least expect it. Grant that I may watch, waiting upon Thee.

15. My Father, I pray that sinners may find peace today. May weary hearts find rest. Strengthen the disappointed and heavily burdened by Thy power. And let me, too, share in Thy favors.

16. Heavenly Father, help me to acknowledge Thy will in the small matters of daily life. Make me faithful in doing them, and enable me to enhance Thy glory in tasks, which seem unimportant. May I consecrate the least as well as the greatest of my efforts to Thee.

17. Merciful Father, I pray for all those in whom sin is stronger than grace. Convince them that Christ is surely greater than the devil and that they can do all things in Him.

18. Holy God, I pray for a more sensitive conscience. Redeem me from the little sins I do not notice. Prevent these from disturbing my precious fellowship with Thee. Purge me from my secret transgressions.

19. Heavenly Father, I beseech Thee that Thou wilt suffuse my heart with Thy peace. Deliver me from anything that might disrupt the spirit of worship in me. Make me quiet in Thy presence.

20. O God, grant that I may glorify every moment of every day. May that day please me, most which bears most fruits for Thee. I would abound in the fruits of goodness, righteousness, and truth.

21. My God and Father, help me to believe that Thou hast the power completely to redeem me. Deliver me from the bondage of evil habits. Grant me the freedom and gladness of Thy saints. May I joyfully go the way of the righteous, and may my soul rejoice in the Lord.

22. Merciful God, I pray for the sick. Remember their many grieves and trials. And make me sympathetic and kind so that I may serve Thee in serving them.

23. Father, I thank Thee that the morning of eternity is dawning, that tedious night is passing, that sorrow will cease and the tears shed in this dark valley will sparkle like dew in the morning sun.

24. Merciful God may my heart in proclaiming Thy praise issue a pure sound. Redeem my life of the discord of murmuring and discontent. May Thy grace grow beautiful in my soul, so that my lips may praise Thy majesty.

25. Savior, direct me to Thy way. Accompany me, instruct me, teach me how to live the Christian life. Help me to keep my eyes fixed steadily upon Thee. So shall I grow in grace.

26. My Father, qualify me for this day's work. May nothing affright me nor anything cause my faith to falter. May I possess a quiet spirit in the Lord and patiently wait upon Him. I know that then all things will be well with me.

27. Merciful Savior, may human mercy bring restoration and courage to many. Replenish the dearth of love that segregates men from each other. May Thy kingdom come. Permit my eyes to see something of the holy brotherly love Thou hest made possible by Thy death.

28. Merciful God, remember me in my work today. I pray that if it be Thy will, Thou wilt make it successful. I would present it to Thee as a sacrifice and would have Thee use it as a means to draw others to Thee.

29. My Lord and Savior, give me Thy peace. Thou knowest how quickly I fear, how every threat frightens me. Keep me calm in storms, and quiet in adversity. I am eager to believe with confidence. Do thou support my frailty.

30. Almighty God, may it suffice me to ask for and seek to fulfill Thy Purpose. Surely, the source of my power is in Thee. Turn me from springs that have no living water. Keep me in Thy communion, O eternal God. Then shall my soul rejoice in gladness.

31. Merciful Father, eagerly I would remember those who grieve. Give me true pity for them. Send Thy Comfort to the ill. May they feel the healing potency of Thy grace. Have compassion upon the anxious and discouraged, and help them to keep the faith.

SEPTEMBER

1. Eternal God, I want my faith to prove fruitful today. Arm me with abundant strength, so that my neighbors may share it with me. Grant me the spirit of self-denial. Make me willing to sacrifice for others when Thou desires it.

2. Merciful Father, sanctify the daily work of all men, in order that it may be profitable for Thy glory. Forbid that we should grow sluggish and indifferent under the burden of our tasks. Make us ever better and more loving. May we be as reverent in our attitude towards our daily business, insignificant as it may be, as we are in our attitude toward prayer.

3. Heavenly Father, let Thy light be my guide as I move through the turmoil of experience. Allow its rays to fall full upon my work. May that light shine radiantly about me whether I scale mountains or walk in valleys, whether I be in prosperity or in adversity. O Heavenly Light, bathe me in Thy rays.

4. My Father, go with me wherever I go. When roads divide before me and I, hesitate to choose, direct me to the way of life and help me to progress upon it.

5. Father, save me from being bitterly disposed. If today I threaten to grow unfriendly and morose, banish the attitude by the sun of Thy love. May meanness and despair be dispelled by the glow of a profound heavenly mindedness.

6. My Father, today I would remember those in Thy presence whom I generally forget. I pray for those I do not love. Safeguard me against self-interest. Hallow my inclinations. Make me merciful. Grant me the pure heart that seeks and recognizes Thy image everywhere.

7. My Lord and Savior, source of all light, do Thou illumine me. Make me a child who loves the light. May I walk in Thy radiance even as Thou dwellest in it.

8. Lord God, the work of another day awaits me. I do not know which cares or benefits it has in store for me. May I begin it with Thee and at no time be deflected to some path that leads away from Thee. I would do Thy will gladly and contentedly.

9. Merciful God, Thou hast promised mankind Thy peace. Teach me to recognize it when I see it. Forbid that I should let the comfort of this world satisfy me. Grant me, instead, the peace that transcends understanding.

10. O God, my Lord, I long for Thee, the bread of life. Engender in me a fervent longing for heavenly gifts. When I grow indifferent, renew in me the ardor of sincere longing for Thee. I would live for righteousness and shun all sin.

11. Father of Grace, may I never forget that I am a child of grace. Keep alive in me the assurance of Thy love. Let me experience Thy nearness and await Thy coming.

12. Almighty God, strengthen my faith, and hope, and love. May I not walk Thy way wearily but with firm and confident steps. May I be one of those who know their calling, who keep their purpose clearly before them, and who look for the appearing of the Master.

13. My Father, grant me the mind of Christ. Take away all my selfish thoughts, and make my sympathies so broad that these will embrace my neighbors.

14. My Father, give me the power to be patient. Free me from irritableness. Redeem me from harsh, unsympathetic words, from selfishness and indifference to others. May I serve my brethren without a thought of myself.

15. My Father, let me walk in Thy light. When I lose sight of Thee, I lose my way. If I can but see Thee as Thou art, I love Thee. Never bar me from looking upon Thy gracious face.

16. Eternal God, I praise Thee. Thy way goes through the deep, dark places, but Thy faith is firm and unmovable as the mountains of God. I thank Thee because I may be sure of Thy loyalty even when I do not feel it. Teach me to know that even the dark clouds are but the disguises of Thy grace.

17. My Father, look down in mercy upon my past life. Forgive me for my unkept vows, my reluctant service, and my frail desire for the truth.

18. Dear Lord, I thank Thee for the children around me. I thank Thee for the gladness they instill into this hard and weary living. I thank Thee for the sunshine which through them is often shed upon weary, grieving souls. May I, too, by often observing them remain young and glad in spirit.

19. Eternal God, illumine my eyes by thy truth. May I see all things in Thy light. Keep me from straying and from erring. Give me the mind of Christ.

20. Holy God, teach me to acknowledge true happiness. Forbid that I should become the prey of worldly arrogance. May I count holiness better than gold. May I passionately pursue heavenly riches until such time as I shall have secured them.

21. Heavenly Father, grant me the strength for the duties of this day. I thank Thee that I may know that I am not asking this of Thee futilely. Arm me for responsibility in Thy strength and grace. Make me believe in Thee with my whole heart. May I walk before and serve Thee with sure confidence.

22. Holy Father, I would humbly wait upon Thee this day. May I acknowledge that Thou comest to me in my joy and in my sadness, in sunshine and in darkness, in rest and labor.

23. Merciful God, I praise Thee for the faithfulness with which Thou lovest me continually. Forgive me my indifference and lack of fervor. Renew the covenant with me. Make me upright and steadfast.

24. Merciful God, teach Thy children the secret of true progress, of growing in the stature of Christ, Thy dear Son. Save us from material ambitions, from pride and selfishness, and make us children of peace. Grant us the holy strength that comes from a firm reliance upon Thee.

25. My Father, enable me to discover Thy voice in the various duties, activities, and events of my daily life.

26. Heavenly Father, teach me to really reach spiritual heights today. Forgive my faults and my indifference. Lend a confidence to my steps, so that I, supported and borne up by Thee, may rise to the plane of a sanctified life.

27. Eternal God may Thy grace release a fountain of consecration in my soul. Deliver me from my self, from foolish arrogance. Make room in my thoughts for my brethren. May all I do be a blessing to them.

28. My Father, keep me bound closely to Thee each hour of this day. Sanctify each moment of my life. Reveal even insignificant things in Thy light so I may see their value.

29. My Father, grant that each time I seek refuge in flight from the tempter I may find a hiding place in Thee. And when I must face him in combat, lend me the strength with which to fight.

30. Heavenly Father, help me to lift up my eyes unto the hills. May I come nearer Thee each day of my life. May the vision of Thy glory grow more vivid with the passing of time. Let me see the Promised Land from afar.

OCTOBER

1. Heavenly Father may I, by looking upon Thee, become like Thee. May I in faith share in Thy abundance. Make me pure in Christ Jesus. I would have my life reveal that I belong to the Almighty God.

2. Eternal God, impart to me the energy I need for my work. Then, so far from performing it in weakness, I shall do it in the strength of the living God. May I rejoice in Thy help and rely wholly upon it, in order that my life may be a continuous hymn of praise.

3. O God of Strength, renew the world by Thy Holy Spirit. Expel vanity and banish conflict from human hearts. Make men fraternally minded; make them pure. May we be one by faith in Christ.

4. Eternal God, send me Thy Holy Spirit today. May He sustain me in all that I do and may His will rule my life.

5. Almighty God, I would praise and exalt Thy name for the hope of eternal life. I thank Thee because Thou dost permit the light of eternity to penetrate life upon earth. I thank Thee because I am not merely dust of the dust, but because Thy divine life also lives in me. Keep me from forgetting to what Thou hast called me.

6. Eternal God, create in me a hunger and thirst after righteousness. May I not be satisfied with a more common aim. Forbid that the longing for things temporal should consume me. Cause my heart to thirst for the fresh springs of water that flow from the fountain of Thy grace.

7. Almighty God, make me faithful in doing Thy duty. Fill me with the spirit of love. Then my yoke will be easy and my burden light. If Thou wilt teach me to see my labor in Thy light, I shall be able to consecrate it to Thee.

8. My Father, protect me from the pollution of the world. Wash me and I shall be clean, my garments white as snow. Sanctify me so that I may live a holy life for Thee.

9. Lord Jesus, Thou art the light of the world. Enable me to walk in it, in order that I may prove profitable for the kingdom.

10. Heavenly Father, make me worthy of Thy adoption of me. May I count all loss, save gaining Christ and becoming like Him. Fill my soul with humility, and place my feet upon the path of Thy commandments.

11. Savior, teach me to bear the cross. Forbid that I should, in selfish impatience, throw off its burden. May I not be sluggish today, but active and zestful. May I hate my life in order to gain mine.

12. Dear Lord, I pray that I may be friendly. Sometimes I roughly grasp the wounds of men in my coarse hands and aggravate their suffering. Give me true sympathy, so that in my feelings I may share the grieves and disappointments of my neighbors. May I help them by touching them with the loving pity of Christ.

13. Merciful God, incline my heart to keeping Thy commandments. Free me from wicked desires. I would earnestly pursue Thy truth and holiness. I would hunger for righteousness. Help me, Almighty One.

14. Merciful Lord, direct my course in life today. Prevent me from taking the first step upon the wrong way. Keep me from seeking this world's happiness. I would retrace the footsteps of my Master.

15. Almighty God, may the power of no enemy subdue Thy light in me. Forbid that temporal cares should dull its radiance. May people everywhere on earth feel Thy life giving rays, O Sun of Righteousness.

16. My Father, purify my thoughts at the beginning of this day. Take away all that is defiled. Direct my eyes to the mountain tops. May my whole life be a following of the upward road.

17. Great and Mighty God, in compassion look down upon my weakness. Fill my impotent heart with the fullness of Thy power. May I share in Thy strength. Grant me the victory and the conflict.

18. Father of Love, I pray for those who still grope upon unknown ways. I pray that Thou wilt let them find Thee. May they sincerely, and because of an eager, inner prompting, learn to do Thy will. Give them, too, a pure heart.

19. Eternal God, may I experience that I am overshadowed by Thy love and grace. Envelope me in Thy goodness. I can go safely, fearlessly, in Thy escort.

20. O Lord, do Thou discipline my words. Hallow what I say. Do Thou by Thy spirit bless my fellowship with others. Keep my tongue, the little, dangerous member, from wickedness. Make me Thy loyal witness.

21. Eternal God, Thy grace is my hope, Thy power my strength. May I seek aid with none but Thee. May I by faith share in Thy divine nature. I would have my dwelling be with Christ in Heaven.

22. Holy Father, completely sanctify me. Let me dedicate my most secret experience, and my innermost thoughts to Thee.

23. Eternal God, I praise Thee. Thy love extends as wide as heaven and envelopes all men. May I constantly keep Thy merciful presence clearly before me. Solace me with the assurance of Thy love, and grant me Thy peace.

24. My Father, make me gracious and sympathetically inclined. Leave room in my heart for my brethren. Forbid that I should push them outside of my thoughts; may I meet them in love and sympathy.

25. Holy God, I would live to Thy honor today. May I do my work as a kind of service designed for and dedicated to Thee. Keep my eyes fixed upon the Son of Man, in order that in all of my conduct I may please Him.

26. My God and Father, teach me to hate what I should hate according to Thy word. May I abhor sin. May I not only dread punishment but really detest what is evil. Keep sin from ever seeming attractive to me; may it, instead, fill me with sadness. I would hate it with a perfect hatred.

27. Lord, I know that I owe everything to Thy grace. Forbid, then, that I should seem indifferent to it. Teach me to know that it is Thy goodness, which gives me temporal and eternal favors. May Thy benefits always draw me nearer Thee.

28. Merciful God, give me the spirit of mercy. Redeem me from an unsympathetic attitude. Make me mild and loving in Thy service, so that the beauty of a life surrendered to Thee may attract others to living it.

29. Eternal God, give me a new and exuberant hope. May I expect great things today and rely upon the promptings of Thy grace for attaining them. May I see Thy miracles today and discover tokens of Thy blessing everywhere.

30. Almighty God, bless me with strength and peace. Let me approach my task as one who is required to give an account of it to His Lord and Master. Keep me, however, from doing my duty from a sense of compulsion.

31. Eternal God, I confess that my hope is Thy grace. Without Thy goodness my life grows impossible. Let me abide in Thy love and see Thy beauty. Grant me the spirit of obedience, so that the secret of the Lord may be mine.

NOVEMBER

1. My Father, I dedicate this new month to Thee. May I appreciate the benefits of being able completely to depend upon Thee. I would taste Thy peace. Give my soul stillness, as it witnesses the love of Christ.

2. Holy Father may all good and true things meet with response from me. When my inner life grows dull, do Thou impart enthusiasm. May I rejoice with the happy and grieve with those who mourn. Keep me bound close to Christ.

3. Almighty God, renew my soul by Thy grace. Let me begin this day in Thy strength. May I fulfill my responsibilities with a victorious faith.

4. Great God, teach me to be meek and lowly. May I never grow harsh in prosperity or bitter in adversity. Fill me with love, and may I steadily rely upon Thee.

5. My Father, I thank Thee for all the favors Thou hast already given me. Keep my memory alive, lest I forget them. May I acknowledge that it is Thy mercy, which has always led me. So may I praise Thee for Thy grace.

6. Father, I pray for the forsaken and rejected. Fill me with love and pity so that I may seek out the bat and point them to Thee. May the example and testimony of my life help them to find the way to the Father's house.

7. My Father, banish every thought that disturbs my communion with and hampers my love of Thee. Open my heart and my thoughts to Thy grace. Then I shall each day praise and glorify Thee.

8. O Lord, my God, what dost Thou desire of me today? What task wouldst Thou have me do? Open my eyes, lest I fail to recognize Thy will. Keep me from squandering this day. I would convert it into eternal gain.

9. Holy Spirit, nurture my inner life to a flourishing growth. Cause the wilderness of my spirit to be a luxuriant garden. Left alone, my life proves barren. Make it beautifully productive. Rejuvenate all things in me today.

10. Father, save me today from the dangers of this world; from an unrestrained temper, from arrogance, greed, and selfishness.

11. Almighty God let Thy love rest upon my spirit, and my love rest in Thee. Forbid that the bond which binds me to Thee should be torn apart. May I in the turmoil of experience, by an unchanging and childlike obedience, stay in close relationship to Thee.

12. My Father and my God, give me the heart of a child. Make me receptive to Thy benefits. May I never lose the sense of wonder and of reverence. Reveal Thy grace anew each day. Lead me from glory to glory. He who loves Thee once finds new treasures in fellowship with Thee continually.

13. Heavenly Father, Thou seest all things. Look down upon me in compassion. Forgive all my sins. Make me thoroughly honest in confessing my transgressions. May I hate them all and positively turn away from them.

14. O my God, teach me to bear my cross without a murmur. Keep me from being a reluctant and unsatisfied follower of Thee. Give me the secret of persevering happily even under heavy burdens. So will Thy strength manifest itself in my weakness.

15. Great and loving God, give me tin one thing
    Thou dost acknowledge as great Give me
    humility, in faith and love. For bid that I
    should follow the great thing of the world
    and so forfeit the crown of life.

16. My Lord and Savior, help me to stay in Thy
    fellowship today. Let me share in Thy
    strength, Thy happiness, Thy rest and
    peace.

17. Father of all men, May I never forget the
    meaning of this, Thy great and glorious
    name. If I would call Thee Father I must
    love all Thy children. I confess that my love
    to these is stinted. Keep me from
    dishonesty in this; give me integrity in
    prayer. Make me pure and true in Thy
    presence.

18. Eternal God, may my feet tread the way of
    Thy commandments. Enable me to serve
    Thee with increasing fervor, lest I go upon
    that way halfheartedly. May I zealously
    pursue the priceless pearl of Thy kingdom,
    promised to those who diligently seek it.

19. Almighty God, safeguard my soul from
    danger. May nothing harm me today, but all
    things prove permanently beneficial. May
    even my enemies be a blessing to me.

20. O Eternal God, May I each day be newly bound to Thee. I would have all I do and all I desire be consecrated to Thee. May the love of Christ fill all my thoughts.

21. God of all mercy, show me the riches of Thy love. Deliver me from selfishness. Make room in me for my neighbors; may many weary travelers find rest and refreshment with me.

22. Eternal God, I live by Thy grace. Make my soul rich and broad, I pray. Save me from a dangerous sense of self sufficiency and from complacency. Fill my heart with a holy longing. Let me not be satisfied until I have become conformed unto Thy image.

23. Eternal Father, teach me how to worship Thee. Enable me to bow before Thee in deep contrition. May I discern Thy presence everywhere, and may the awareness of it fill me with holy humility. Teach me to pray.

24. Gracious Savior, purify my soul by Thy holy word. Banish every thought that is alien to Thee. Make my heart a temple of light and peace. May Thy precious blood be my sole appeal in life and death.

25. My Father, do Thou reign over all my days. I would begin them as Thou wouldst have me, and conclude them with faith in Thy forgiving race. May Thy light be shed abroad over my life until the end.

26. O Spirit of Grace, may I never forget and never despise Thee. Never allow me to determine a matter without asking Thy counsel and direction. I beseech Thee to dispel the darkness in me and make me a more perfect embodiment of a child of light.

27. Heavenly Father, help me to keep my eyes upon Thee uninterruptedly today. May things mean and base not draw them down. Enable me to walk as a child of the Almighty, who knows that his inheritance in eternity is carefully preserved.

28. My Father, help me to hear Thy voice when it speaks to me, and to respond to it eagerly. May I gladly obey even when it directs me to difficult duties. Help me to take up Thy cross and to follow Thee.

29. My Father, redeem me from my besetting sin. Deliver me from all evil desires. Change my inclinations so completely that I may desire nothing outside of Thee. I would drink at the fountain of Thy joy until I am fully satisfied.

30. My Father, I thank Thee for all that have already entered into Thy rest. May my sure expectation of heavenly glory inspire me for temporal activity. May my daily work be the building of an altar for Thee; may all I do be a sacrifice which pleases Thee.

DECEMBER

1. My Savior, do Thou by grace give me Thy mind and let me ever be more intimately associated with Thee. Save me from every thought that wars against Thee. Lead me, lest I stray, and so cause others to leave Thee.

2. Eternal God, look upon me in compassion and let Thy mercy release abundant streams of sympathy. May I reflect the image of my Master. May His love fill my life and his sacrifice make me willing to sacrifice for others.

3. Father of all mercies, comfort me so that I may solace others. May I dispense with my hidden treasures, all gifts of Thy grace, sharing them eagerly with my neighbors.

4. Heavenly Father, I am weak. Make me strong by Thy grace. May I in every way be successful in completing my work today. Let me go about it eagerly. May I be victor over the Evil One in every combat, conquering in Him who loves me.

5. Eternal God, only in Thy light can I safely go upon my way. May I not become the victim of self direction and grope in darkness. I would hunger for Thy Word and be led by it in life.

78

6. My Father, convert every disappointment I experience into blessing. May I be essentially at peace even in defeat, by keeping my hope fixed upon Thee. May all my adversities glorify Thee at last.

7. Holy Spirit, reinvigorate my energies. Inspire new loyalty in my soul. Keep my faith from blighting in the bud. Let it blossom and bear fruit.

8. My Father, give me a true appreciation of Thy way. Then I shall see Thee in things commonplace, and in all that happens to me I shall be able to discover Thy will.

9. My heavenly Father, Thou art the fountain of life. Each time I forget that my spirit dies. Constantly renew it by Thy strength. May I ever return to the source and drink there of the water of life. Savior, give me to drink.

10. My Father, rule over desires, and make them subservient to Thy will. May they bow in reverence to Thy purposes and never assert themselves arrogantly in contention against Thee.

11. O my Father in Heaven, make me like little children. Keep me from pride; give me simplicity. May I never be ashamed of leaning upon Thee, or of begging at the gates of Thy temple daily.

12. Eternal God, my life is the gift of Thy goodness. Let me walk in Thy gracious light today, so that I may be wholly filled with Thy comfort.

13. O God, merciful Father, I pray for those who have strayed far from the Father's house. Have compassion upon the rejected of men. Induce many to help them, and do Thou thyself attract those who are miserable to Thy paternal heart. Point their faces to the light. Cleanse them of their sins.

14. Great God, give that I may fear nothing this day can present to me. Be Thou my refuge so that I may await events quietly and in confidence.

15. Eternal God, I would really know the Christ. Do not abandon me to my own folly. Thou knowest my limitations. Shed divine light upon my soul. Make me strong in Christ Jesus.

16. Heavenly Father, help me to understand why Thou hast sent me so much adversity. Teach me to know that suffering and trials also are my friends. Convert my temporal disappointments into eternal benefits.

17. Almighty God lift my life to the plane of Thy light. Forbid that I should Choose some human calculation as my standard. I would willingly keep Thy commandments. Help me to witness for Thy truth wherever I may be.

18. Holy Spirit, spirit of mercy, descend upon all men. Deliver them from fear and error, and direct their hearts to the way of light and truth. May we all discern the influence of Thy grace in our souls.

19. Father, receive me anew into Thy fellowship. Keep me from indifference and from manifesting only the externalities of religion. May I instead, by the conquering power of Thy love, always reveal that I am in intimate communion with Thee.

20. Merciful Father, Thou knowest my sins. Help me to abhor them. I lay them bare before Thee. I would love only the good, and pursue only the pure and holy things.

21. God of all grace, May Thy Holy Spirit work upon my soul and penetrate its secret Places. Forbid that I should hide anything; let me present my whole self willingly to Thee. Try my heart and desires and make me mine.

22. My Father, I would have my faults teach me and admonish me. May yesterday's folly by Thy grace make me wise today.

23. Great God, keep me from thinking unworthily of Thee. May Thy love and holiness be the really great things in my life. Then I shall be rich and holy.

24. My Father, I thank Thee for the privilege of seeing Thy face in Christ Jesus. May I love Thy countenance. May I care to discern Thy footsteps, to acknowledge all Thy approaches to me.

25. Lord Jesus Christ, my dear Savior, this is Thy birthday. I would honor and praise Thee in it. Show me how to appear before Thee. Give me the spirit of humble reverence, in order that I may see the Mystery of Thy beauty. So may today be a festival for my soul.

26. Almighty Lord, Lord of spirits, may we see Thy features plainly in the face of Jesus, whose birthday we remembered. Give us a vital awareness of Thy presence. Shed the light of Thy countenance upon us. Then will we rejoice in Thee.

27. Father of Grace, again I pray that Thou wilt send the light of Thy countenance upon us. May it engender in us a firm faith and pure desires. Fill our hearts with love for Thy truth.

28. King of Honor. Lord of Glory, give me open eyes for a heavenly, an eternal life. Let me acknowledge it whenever it appears on earth. Direct my eyes to the things above. Even here make me a child of eternity.

29. My risen Lord and Savior, let me taste Thy peace. So easily I am discouraged and frightened and yet I eagerly long for abiding rest. Grant me Thy peace. Help me to trust in Thee for time and for eternity.

30. Almighty God, Thy power is my shield. I rely upon Thee in the battle against the world, the flesh, and the devil. Support my helplessness by Thy strength.

31. Heavenly Father, may this year be commended to Thy love and race. Convert all inadequacies and transgressions to benefits, and forgive all my guilt. I thank Thee and praise Thee for every victory which Thou has given me. Keep me humble, Father: may I expect nothing from myself and all from Thee. I pray that I may end the year in Thy peace.

Made in the USA
Middletown, DE
13 August 2020

15248236R00050